A Thorn in the Flesh

D1334329

A Thorn in the Flesh

Selected Poems

~~EDDIE LINDEN~~

To ERNE. We FirsT met in
1960 in HempSTead
BesT wishes

Foreword by James Campbell

Eddie Linden;
January the 18th/1/2012.

Hearing Eye

Published by Hearing Eye 2011

Hearing Eye, Box 1, 99 Torriano Avenue
London NW5 2RX, UK
email: hearing_eye@torriano.org
for book orders: books@hearingeye.org
www.hearingeye.org

ISBN: 978-1-905082-63-6

—ɷ—

Hearing Eye is represented by
Inpress Ltd in the UK – see www.inpressbooks.co.uk
Trade distribution: Central Books, Hackney Wick, London E9 5LN

—ɷ—

Cover portrait of Eddie Linden by Gerald Mangan
Designed by Martin Parker at www.silbercow.co.uk
Printed by Aldgate Press, London

Foreword

James Campbell

One recent Christmas Day in Hampstead, Eddie Linden sat quietly through lunch while others argued and reminisced all around him, speaking only to compliment the hostess or recall past seasonal outings to Ireland. When the plates were cleared away, however, and he was asked if he would recite a few poems, Eddie Linden came to life.

Anyone who has witnessed one of these performances is unlikely to forget it. Other poets recite from memory, but few bring to the job the kind of "attack" that Eddie does. He took to the floor, and with eyes closed and head tilted ever so slightly upward began to speak his most famous poem:

> A woman roars from the upper window
> "They're at it again, Maggie!
> Five stitches in our Tommy's face, Lizzie!
> Eddie's in the Royal wi' a sword in his stomach
> and the razor's floating in the River Clyde."

A *sword* in his stomach? (The "Eddie" of the poem is distinct from the author.) Yes, gang members in Glasgow before and after the Second World War did carry swords – and machetes. A "hatchet man" in the Clydeside context meant what it said. Much of the violence was directed at members of one religious group by those of another – "walls scrawled with FUCK THE POPE and / blue-lettered words GOD BLESS THE RANGERS", as the poem evokes it. The existence of this sectarian split, and the anxieties it intensified in his own head, was one of the reasons that Eddie fled the West of Scotland in the 1960s and moved to London.

Not the only reason, though. There was also his appalling upbringing – a history of rejection that Dickens might have chosen to tone down – and the tussles with drink and sex that appear to have stemmed from it.

The next poem Eddie read that Christmas was "The Miner", eight lines of pure feeling dedicated to "my father", whom he scarcely knew: "Your face has never / moved . . ."; never moved, that is, from the poet's inner eye. Sometimes, when reciting, Eddie clasps a hand to his forehead, or takes a few steps forward or back. But the eyes stay closed . . .

> and many men are buried here
> whose shadows linger on.

Some people reading *A Thorn in the Flesh* will be familiar with a scene such as this one. For those unacquainted with Eddie Linden, however – and I hope this book will bring him many new readers – I would like to add another important detail.

When Eddie arrived in the South (even those who have met him only once will always know him as "Eddie"), he had difficulties with the alphabet. Which way round was a word spelled? Why did it not look right when written down? Gradually, he took hold of one particular letter, and alchemized it into his own precious medium of communication. The letter was "A" and the medium was *Aquarius*, the magazine of poetry, fiction and reviews which was launched in 1969, and hasn't reached dry dock yet. "Starting the magazine brought an absolute stability into my life", he told me recently. He felt that if he had had an ordinary upbringing, he might have been a schoolteacher. "I might not even be running the magazine. I just lived for it. The thing that saved me – this creative thing – it changed my whole life."

Many of the poems in this book were published in Eddie's first collection, *City of Razors* (1980). Twenty others have been added. The dominant feeling is a sense of loss – the loss of something that was never his. And yet they are free of bitterness. Eddie is one of the most honest people I know, and one of those most sincere. Several verses here came into being as tributes to those who have shown him kindness, or have bolstered his love of literature: Father Michael Hollings, for example, or John Heath-Stubbs, another poet obliged to recite from memory. Eddie's effort to grasp the blind poet's plight, in "A Man in Bayswater", is full of imaginative sympathy:

> Sunshine, darkness in his eyes
> Children in the streets . . .

Feeling to the bar
Thinking glass and Guinness.

Others have written sympathetically of Eddie, in turn. Among the contributors to *Eddie's Own Aquarius* (2005), an issue of the magazine devoted to its founder, were Alan Brownjohn, Seamus Heaney, Tom Leonard and Peter Porter.

The tribute that sticks in my mind, however, dates from thirty years earlier. It came from the American poet Robert Creeley, and was prompted by Eddie's over-enthusiasm, perhaps skidding along on the contents of "glass and Guinness", during Creeley's reading at the Cambridge Poetry Festival. I was present, a student down from Edinburgh, an admirer of the Black Mountain poet but not yet a familiar of the editor of *Aquarius*. The collision of Creeley's sotto voce nervous ejaculations and Eddie's cries of support from the gallery – as if from the football terraces that echo behind "City of Razors" – was memorable. On opening Creeley's next collection, *Later*, I found a poem called "Thanks". It begins with a hearty "Here's to Eddie", the rare being who "Takes on the burden / Of your confusions". The encounter left a deep impression on Creeley:

> I won't escape
> His conversation
> But will listen as I've learned to,
>
> And drink
> And think again
> With this dear man
> Of the true, the good, the dead.

Creeley died in 2005. If he had had the opportunity to read *A Thorn in the Flesh*, or to hear Eddie deliver some of its contents, he would have been glad to listen again. "And think again."

Acknowledgements:

Of the poems in this selection, 17 were published in *City of Razors and other poems*
(Jay Landesman Ltd, 1980)
Over the years, some of those and other pieces have appeared in various publications,
including *The Irish Times*, *The Fortnight*, *Tribune*, *Guardian*, *Morning Star*, *Ulster Tatler*,
and the anthologies: *The Best of Scottish Poetry... contemporary Scottish verse*
(ed. Robin Bell, Chambers, 1989)
The Poolbeg Book of Irish Poetry for children (ed. Shaun Traynor, Poolbeg, 1979)
The Penguin Book of Homosexual Verse (ed. Stephen Coote, Penguin, 1983,1986)
Life Doesn't Frighten Me At All (ed. John Agard, Heinemann, 1989)
In the Company of Poets (ed. John Rety, Hearing Eye, 2003)
Well Versed (ed. John Rety, Hearing Eye, 2009)
and *Eddie's Own Aquarius* (ed. Constance Short and Anthony Carroll,
Cahermee Publications, 2005)

—⚛—

For this book, there have been minor changes in some pieces.

A number of the poems have not appeared in print previously.

Poems by Eddie Linden have been translated into
French, Irish, Spanish, Russian and Finnish.

Contents

In memory of

John Rety
publisher
of Hearing Eye

and

John Ezard
journalist
of the *Guardian*

The Little Flower

Gently it moves
And bends with the wind.
His eyes wonder at
All the lovely things around him.
The need to touch, feel
The strange discovery registering in
The unconscious part of his mind.
He will remember
And these will be his thoughts
When dreams return
In manhood
Then he will find
The little flower
And know.

Passing Youth

I was two and remember
Thirty-two years later
And cried like the day
He left her womb
Lost, but found in a
Wood covered in green
And every day he walked
Down by the river
Looking for the nest
Bathing in the river
To the sounds of birds
Coming in his direction
His heart felt warm
As he held the child
In his arms
Then he remembered
His mother by the bed
And Teddy under the tree
With lights, Christmas
Snow on the slag-hills
The little finger-mark on the frosted window-pane
Then summer
And child had gone
School and teacher
At his desk,
Plates of sand
And Big Bad Wolf
Ring of Roses in
The park, swings
Of joy and moonlight nights
Rapping doors and overturned bins,
Cobbled streets
Gas lamps, cracked roof
With sandstone
Houses and then rain

And thunder brought him
Back to himself, to the youth
In the mirror, changed with the years
But feeling young
In the company of the boy
With dark blue eyes
And a poet's face,
Wanting what could not be bought,
Failing to see
With the passing of time, withered tree
Shedding its leaves
As the child went past.

Two Bastards

for David Leitch,
author of 'God Stand Up For Bastards'

This drive within me
pushes me on. I cannot
stop now. Looking back
tells us nothing. Even
that RTE broadcast did not
produce Daddy. Mother
has the secret and
it's buried in Glasgow.
Terry's in Crossmaglen
with memories of Springburn.
Who's the one in the photo,
was he from Dundalk?
I've travelled much in
cities far away – Edmonton,
Calgary, Toronto and
New York where they talk of
being Irish on March the 17th.
What's all this green
crap got to do with you?
I'll meet you in Dublin
on July the 12th. Drive on taxi,
Maida Vale will do me.

Landscape

Driven by nostalgia
across an upturned landscape
I venture with fear and trepidation
back into the womb of time,
searching for a cord to link
the present with the past.
My head lurches out of the window of the carriage
as it passes Bellshill station,
I look into the faces of passengers
that might tell me where we have met,
that will tell me a message.
I try to reconstruct the jigsaw puzzle
in my mind
or catch a smell that will link me with
a period buried below a highway road,
but by the time I reach my destination
a ticket collector reminds me
that I am in Cambuslang.

The Nest

The echo of the burn as it runs yellow
And dark blue slag on the pit surface
Reminded him of his past.
The wheel of life sounded its
Message of time.
The blast of death
Rang its bells in the hearts of the homes.
The grim face in the mirror
Faded with time into the slag heaps
From where he came.
The moon revealed its ugly village houses.
A dog howled its death-like sound,
A baby cried from the cold of night,
A father knelt in
The bowels of the earth, waiting for light
In darkest hell, where he never saw.
Only winter remained,
And nothing returned to the nest in the tree
But the snow that covered
The world of his past.

The Miner

for my Father

Your face has never
moved, it still contains
the marks of toil, deep in
blue. These slag heaps
now in green have
flowers instead of dust
and many men are buried here
whose shadows linger on.

Ave Maria

On a stormy night
As I tossed and tumbled
And tried to think,
I remembered my first Holy Communion:
And that plastic ornament
And that halo of electric bulbs,
Would repulse any thought of holiness.
Wrapped up, my mind reverted to childhood memories,
Trying to trample that unrealistic
Madonna of clay,
Real
And radiating
With the warmth of the sun,
Its rays penetrating
With a spiritual tranquillity
That imprisoned me
In affection.
And the birds were whistling in the distance
As we sipped our tea
And said: Ave Maria,
        Ave Maria.

An Irish Birthright

James Glackin, my uncle

Yet it was from a torn
and divided land,
fatherless but with one
sister, mother and two
brothers. Ready to recreate
with all the strength within you,
to dig again as
others of the family line
had done,
and to a Scotland ravaged
by recession. Start afresh
with faith and hope,
a banner platform within your soul.
Faced with hunger, want and
poverty and on you went putting together
the broken pieces, building anew around
the family shell. Proud, but firm in belief
in your aim of serving your Irish God
that had protected you through ages past.
The red-hot metal that gave you bread
and men you served so well
will make notes for later records.
The deeds that mark your time
and day now turn to recollect
in tranquil summers' days and
see your son rejoice in Mass
at Carfin grotto.

The Slum

There's not much sun ever gets through
Winter or summer.
The roof is cracked
And the wall oozes its continuous sweat.
A worm is worming her way though life,
She's only thirty
With the unborn inside –
Seems to have been on the move
From one den to another:
Ten years in a dirt-box, and the little animals
Have never seen a bath.
It always rains, inside and outside.
Her life goes on,
Waiting for the day when the door will open
And the sun will shine –
Not as long as that bastard's on the door-knob.
The mean street with ragged children
Dog-shit and broken glass.
The fuzz crawling around
As if protecting the slums.
At night they clear the air with violence.
Beer helps to forget the mess.
Then there's the black boy: he starts the thunder,
With much the same self-pity.
They can't see they're in the same boat
In this hungry palace
Full of hungry faces,
Objects waiting to be delivered
From this dump, and moved
Into a larger dump
That's far too steep to look down,
Much colder than the pavements they left twelve months ago.

City of Razors

for the city of Glasgow

Cobbled streets, littered with broken milk bottles,
reeking chimneys and dirty tenement buildings,
walls scrawled with FUCK THE POPE and
blue-lettered words GOD BLESS THE RANGERS.

Old woman at the corner, arms folded, babe in pram,
a drunk man's voice from the other pavement,
And out come the Catholics from evening confessional;

A woman roars from the upper window
"They're at it again, Maggie!
Five stitches in our Tommy's face, Lizzie!
Eddie's in the Royal wi' a sword in his stomach
and the razor's floating in the River Clyde."

There is roaring in Hope Street,
They're killing in the Carlton,
There's an ambulance in Bridgeton,
And a laddie in the Royal.

Misfits

Just dregs at the bottom of the barrel.
Look at his mouth
See how fast he consumes his meal.
The table is bare like him.
He warms his hands
And gratefully accepts the tea.
Memories of better days flood his mind
As his conversation darts back into the past
Because there is no future
Only the mean streets
And channels of dog-ends.

The Man in the Black Suit

He didn't want me to ask too many questions
The coffee warmed his cold body
His Glasgow accent was clear
The black suit gave away the secret
of what he had done in the past.
The drink had reduced his spirit for life
It was all in the face.
The shoes years old
A torn prayerbook in his pocket.

Drag Show

Walking through a lonely bar
full of hungry faces,
On stage she danced
through a sea of smoke,
While men mocked and laughed
at her act. Her eyes told you
everything:
Pain that travelled through
every vein, with dead music
and cheap jokes.

Night Time in a City

I walk with rain
singing in my ears
damp streets and shadows
ideas dancing through my mind
what of tomorrow?
Can it be done?
The all-night café
The dregs of the night
dirty floors
mucky cigarette ends
waiters with thin waists
holding coffee cups
music-box with messages for the lonely.
Then to the quiet street
with its figures loitering for trade
old men wrapped in paper in shop doorways.
Night time in the city is over
I must return to my bed of dreams.

Sleepless Night

Long nights and only a book;
A letter can kill an hour
A bath, a shave can wear
An hour. The clock ticks
Three with time to come;
Sleep impossible. The pill wore
Off. Morning drifting in.
The birds begin to sing
The dreams of what's to come
And out of bed we get.
The milkman rings the bell.
The postman starts the day.

Prayers for the Foetus

Thanks for inviting me to your table
Surrounded by the instruments of the Catholic Church
And that nun resenting the lady that had an abortion
And they all talked about the prayer meetings
And how much hot tea was given at the door.
The sacrifice of the mass
And the prayers for the foetus thrown in the bin
And then he said 'Go in peace'
And the altar boy had an erection
And the mass is over
And the supper is over
And they picked up the baby and took it home.

To Archbishop Roberts

You were a beacon to my life.

In the cradle of my catholicity
I, who played like all children
With philosophy and ideas, trying
To reconcile the Body of Christ with the earth,

Was imprisoned in a dogma of faith;
While clouds of freedom
Flowed from the balcony
Of that majestic saint John XXIII.

Innocence still reigned in my mind
And from that brief moment conflict emerged
Yet unsolved in this tarnished world
Raging against the atom fumes
And into the arena did you appear.

You who would not wear temporal power
Nor wear the rings that glitter in the sun
Your only wish that he might hear your plead
Eccling as Luther did in centuries gone by.

You, a true conscience
Pleading your cause among the silent shepherds
Amid a world of changing values,
Will not have stopped the march of time.

I, in cynicism and despair feel compassion
For men like you.
I lost in a sea of confusion

Now doubt the rock of Peter.
It might be that I am lost among the corn
Yet wait for the day when a glare of light
Might point the way,
Finding the sanctuary and tranquillity

That you, on your eightieth year, have found.

A Table of Fruit

for Father Michael Hollings

Your table contains everything.
You and everyone share Christ.
Faith and prayer are part of the day.
Time and space are made possible.
Nothing will distract you from your purpose or plans
Even when you are not there.

Quiet are your ways
But your message gets through.
Your trees bear fruit.
You see to your garden in a practical way,
Nor do you harass your workers,
Only guide their hands.

Everything is carefully placed in time
For Mass; when they arrive you will be there
Carrying the bread and wine.

Is God a Protestant?

When I last saw you
in Belfast, you asked me
the same question,
one we can never
resolve. We talked
about culture difficulties,
our divided lives, our
History, and God
was never far away.
You talked about King
Billy and I about
Orange and Green.
An hour later a bomb
went off near the
Crown Bar. You finished
your drink just as the
barman called Time.
I forgot to ask did you
hear the news from
Glasgow, Rangers signed
a Catholic.

A Sunday in Cambridge

That Sunday was like an unfinished dream.
I've never been able to get it out of my mind.
You looked like Mary Magdalen
And I wanted to wash your feet.
The more I looked into your eyes
The stronger the pain.
Your thin body and small waist
Were all I wanted to possess,
But a shadow hovering in our midst
Prevented a possible communion.

Where Lovers Never Meet

Silent they walk
Hidden by masks of fear.

There are no angels here
Nor rays of light
Even the moon that white-eyed nurse
Would scare the loveless birds away.

Heartless men in need of love
Will kill the love by three
And on they search
As if no end in sight.

Only the light will
Kill the joy of night
In a place
Where lovers never meet.

A Drunken Egotist

Morning sun
Ticking clock
Dirty cups
Musty room
Ringing 'phone
Stale milk bottles
like a stale mouth.

Sunday *Observer*
Sunday Times
Bacon and egg
tea and toast

Walk in the park
Man on the platform
Woman on a bench
Evening in bar
Drink in his glass
Swivering head
Struggling on stairs
Falling in bath
Falling on bed.

Hampstead by Night

Comfortable little suburb north of London
with its wooded heath
where queers and heteros nest at night
Little girls in mini-skirts
Boys with long hair and pockets full of French letters
preparing for a night's fucking
Pubs flowing with artists
conversing about their masterpieces
not yet on canvas
Playwrights with introductions to the latest play
that they plan to write in their bedsitters
Writers with unfinished novels
Poets reciting their newest poems
that only find a hearing in the Rosslyn Arms
or Leonie's parlour in Downshire Hill
Middle-class civil servants off duty
dressed in jeans for the weekend rest
Middle-class ladies hoping for parties and men with big pricks
Public schoolboys with effeminate looks
hoping to win the hearts of butcher boys from Islington and Camden
While the comfortable bourgeois hide in their castles
on the top of the hill
And the rest of the bourgeoisie amuse themselves
in the village two stops from Camden Town.

Court Jester

How he looks at me
makes me burn inside.
Fuck I've had as much
as I can take you bastard.
Love is what you need.
What is it going to look
like in forty years from now?
The pain, the fear from
day to day. Waiting for
the letter that never comes.
He sits there dropping poets'
names until one becomes
drunk and cannot hear
or see. Will someone rid me
of this pest that lingers
in our midst. O Christ take
away this painful fool.

Editor

So you run a magazine?
Ah, that's right.
Who do you publish?
Cunts that think
They're geniuses: poets.
It's a craft so they tell me.
The postman hates me
Ye understand why,
And those poor bastards
Get upset if they're
Left out.
There's nae money in this
Game, but literary parties
Where every cunt cuts each
Other up. *This is not the trade*
For you Jimmy, if a wis you
I'd go back to the pit. Why?
Because you meet real people.

After the Reading

we moved on
into a Flat
full of people with well-fed faces
drinking Red Wine
being very Intellectual
and Nice. Behind
their hidden faces lay
a smile too difficult
to make out.
Then the poet arrived,
fully clothed,
only to find
vultures
ready to strip him down
mentally, and
leave him naked to the world.
What have you found
underneath his flesh?
Nothing.
Then for godsake
Leave him alone.

To Robert Burns

'A fig for those by law protected!
Liberty's a glorious feast
Courts for cowards were erected,
Churches built to please the priest.'

The day I attended your grave
I found that, like Christ's, your followers had removed
Your literary bones.
I remembered your words 'A poet's fame is in his grave.'
Even the king had sent a letter, a little late.

Robert, you must hate the twenty-fifth
When haters of literature get together
To mark your name
And disturb your peace.
What would those good bankers have said
When you called for revolution?

Your place in history is with those who understood the word,
Those kings of poetry before your time cannot be left for Philistines
who forget Hogg, Fergusson, Ramsay, Henryson, Dunbar.

The Stone Bear in Elizabeth Smart's Garden

No more will we see you,
or the place where you remained
a stone for many a year.
So has gone the creator of
the garden that was called
a poem. Elizabeth, without
you there could be nothing. Gone
is the love that overwhelmed
the presence of everything.
The books that covered the house,
and your spirit, and your warmth
radiated everything.
The Bear that saw it all
if only it could speak
what stories it would tell.
They will remain a memory when
The Dell is long forgot.

A Man in Bayswater:
John Heath-Stubbs

Sunshine, darkness in his eyes
children in the streets
as he gropes his way ahead

Cracking staircase
running cistern

Passing motors
safely does he walk
hitting stick and pavement

Feeling to the bar
Thinking glass and Guinness
Listening to the voices
Mind in distant wander
Lighted pipe and smoke
circling in the air

Retiring to his *casa*
And to a bed of dreams.

The Concert

for Lloyd Orchard

Music is what he lives by
He directs his pen and we wait for the finished piece
The subject he has thought long
His time is limited
Do not distract him until he calls back.
From outside his room comes the sound of music,
You know he's getting there, he will call a taxi
And deliver the end product.

The vodka bottle is back on the table and the concert goes on.

For a Dublin Artist

for John Behan

He works in bronze creating matter in steel
Not like those who sit in judgment with jars of Guinness,
I have seen them on high stools passing out unpublished work
While someone labours into the night amid the lightning flash
   of a welder's rod:

His is not just of brain as of brawn
Nor do you find a man in idle talk with fools in intellectual bars
Only in the gallery will you find the finished piece
And find the man.

For Philippe Jamet

Our last meeting in Paris
Was short, the memory of you
Remains in my mind,
And each visit to Paris
Brings it back. I walk
The streets of Paris, but there's
Little chance of finding you.
What would I say
If we should meet? It's twenty years
Since we last talked,
And so much water has flowed
Down the Seine
That would have washed away
So much of the youth
You had in London. My youth
Has long faded, and all
That's left is a memory of you
In that bedsit world
Of Maida Vale.

In Memory of James Glackin

'Do not go gentle into that good night'

You went on a
Christmas day,
your own Holy Day.
You didn't forget
me.
I was in Dundalk
when the phone
rang with your
message. Thanks
for arranging with the
Holy Spirit that the boat
from Ireland would be in time
for me to hear
Mass before
your long holiday.
No doubt
you have had a reunion with the family;
how's Granny?
Tell Uncle Paddy I've
got a great book
Greyhound for Breakfast
I am sure he can get it from
God's library.
And my last request – tell
Mother not
to forget to say
a novena for her
mad son Eddie.

The Candle in the Country

for Avril Bernadette Glackin

I was not there when you arrived
But sensed you in my thoughts.
Like you, I too arrived –
But much more complicated
With a mark that scarred my body,
Invisible, but obvious.
Now you are here to stay with us
And face the winds from east to west,
To face the storm and rains of life
That will beset your little soul:

The flowers will bloom as they do wither,
The flowers of your eternalness,
But mine is yet a withered one,
That fails to yield the fruit.
And you will walk along the street,
And they will bid you day.
And the candle that shines with a crimson reflection
Will be your light for life.

Tranquillity

for Douglas Hyde on his eightieth birthday

It started with a letter
Later a phone call from a London box
Inspired by a moving autobiography.
A meeting near Kings Cross on a cold
Wet night in winter '58
Relating experiences on the road
from Aldermaston as people talked of genocide.
Young men's dreams –
Priests trying to work out peace.
Socialism, mass communion, sleeping in schools
or some good person's floor.
Songs never to be forgotten.
You will remember cities where I have never been.
Your active pen that painted words in papers.
Truth in a planet up for obliteration.
Douglas, may I be your birthday guest
And share your tranquil memories.

1991

Peace

Let us walk
among the trees
and think of days
long far away.

Let us walk
among the trees
and play the games
we played when young.

Let us walk
among the trees
and think of things
we often thought.

Let us walk among
the trees
and look for things
that must be true.

Let us walk
among the trees
and find the answer
to our pain.

Let us walk among
the trees
and find the peace
we long to have.

Breaking Bread

Everything is kept in time
and history is marked into the stones.
This is where it all began,
under the hot sun.
St Paul laid the foundations. A priest
sits and drinks with the villagers.
An old man with a face baked by the sun
walks in the shade.
We take our wine and brandy
and look down into the valley
with thoughts in distant places.
A cloud above the mountain warns
of the coming blackness that will blot out
this ancient civilisation.
Nothing will remain but
To break bread and give thanks.

Near Kopanaki, Greece. August 1986